DEBATING THE ISSUES

Legalizing Marijuana

Marne Ventura

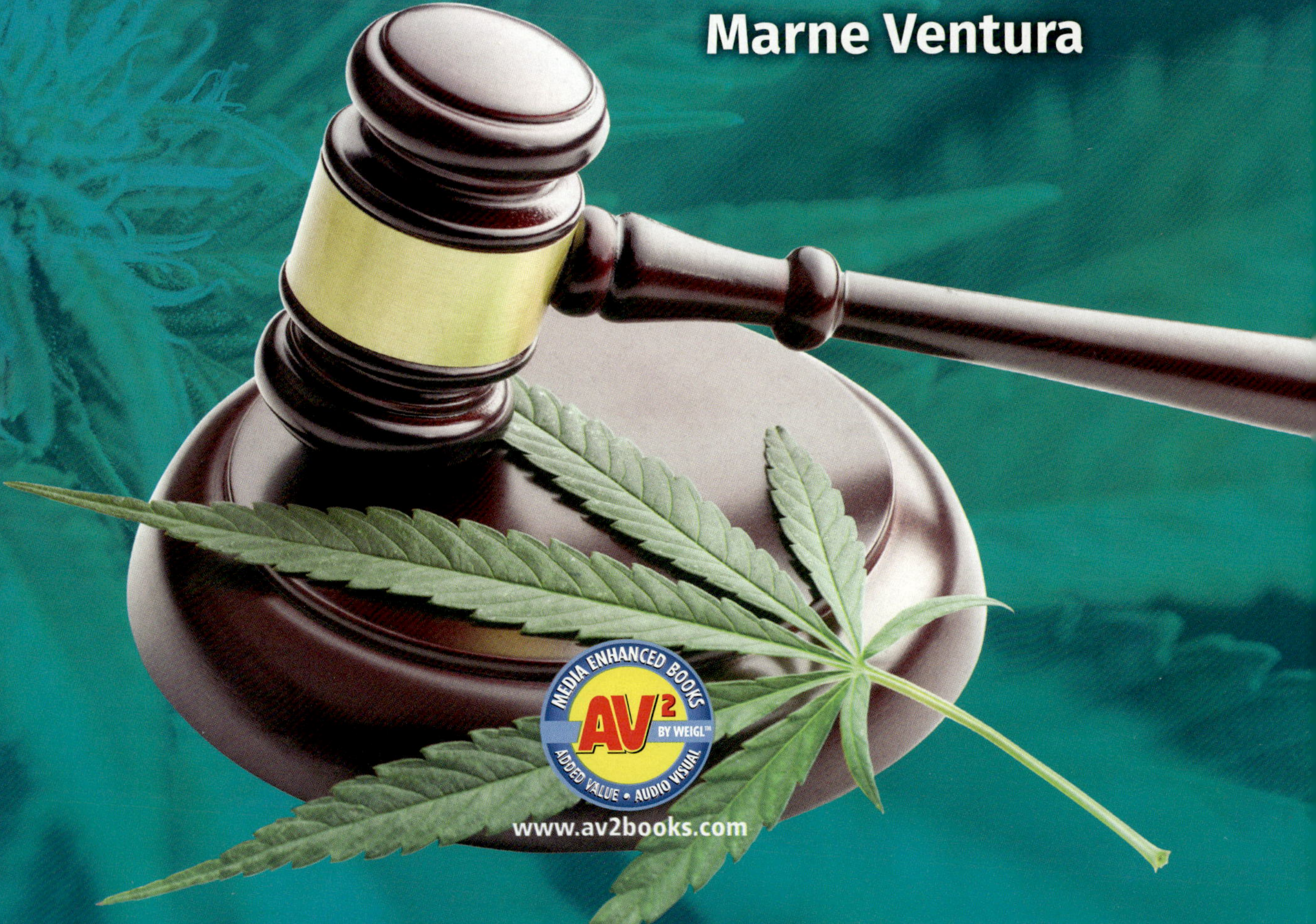

MEDIA ENHANCED BOOKS AV² BY WEIGL ADDED VALUE • AUDIO VISUAL

www.av2books.com

AV² provides enriched content that supplements and complements this book. Weigl's AV² books strive to create inspired learning and engage young minds in a total learning experience.

Go to www.av2books.com, and enter this book's unique code.

BOOK CODE

AVL62577

AV² by Weigl brings you media enhanced books that support active learning.

Your AV² Media Enhanced books come alive with...

Audio
Listen to sections of the book read aloud.

Key Words
Study vocabulary, and complete a matching word activity.

Video
Watch informative video clips.

Quizzes
Test your knowledge.

Embedded Weblinks
Gain additional information for research.

Slide Show
View images and captions, and prepare a presentation.

Try This!
Complete activities and hands-on experiments.

... and much, much more!

Published by AV² by Weigl
350 5th Avenue, 59th Floor New York, NY 10118
Website: www.av2books.com

Library of Congress Cataloging-in-Publication Data

Names: Ventura, Marne, author.
Title: Legalizing marijuana / Marne Ventura.
Description: New York, NY : AV2 by Weigl, [2019] | Series: Debating the issues | Includes index.
Identifiers: LCCN 2018053454 (print) | LCCN 2018055556 (ebook) | ISBN 9781489696014 (Multi User Ebook) | ISBN 9781489696021 (Single User Ebook) | ISBN 9781489695994 (hardcover : alk. paper) | ISBN 9781489696007 (softcover : alk. paper)
Subjects: LCSH: Drug legalization--United States--Juvenile literature. | Marijuana--Law and legislation--United States--Juvenile literature. | Marijuana abuse--United States--Juvenile literature. | Marijuana--United States--Juvenile literature.
Classification: LCC HV5825 (ebook) | LCC HV5825 .V46 2019 (print) | DDC 362.2950973--dc23
LC record available at https://lccn.loc.gov/2018053454

Printed in the United States of America in Brainerd, Minnesota
1 2 3 4 5 6 7 8 9 0 22 21 20 19 18

122018
112318

First published by North Star in 2018

Project Coordinator: Priyanka Das Designer: Ana María Vidal

Every reasonable effort has been made to trace ownership and to obtain permission to reprint copyright material. The publishers would be pleased to have any errors or omissions brought to their attention so that they may be corrected in subsequent printings.

Weigl acknowledges Getty Images, iStock, Shutterstock, Newscom, and Alamy as its primary image suppliers for this title.

Legalizing Marijuana

Contents

Growers dry marijuana plants by hanging them upside down.

The Basics of Marijuana

Humans have used marijuana since ancient times. Farmers in Central Asia and India grew marijuana thousands of years ago. Today, marijuana is grown all over the world.

Marijuana is the name for the dried leaves and flowers of the cannabis plant. Cannabis plants contain more than 400 chemicals. These chemicals have many uses. For example, doctors **prescribe** medical marijuana to treat pain.

Some people use marijuana for **recreational** purposes. They might smoke a marijuana cigarette or eat foods containing marijuana. Chemicals in marijuana can make users feel happy and relaxed. This feeling is called a high.

Laws on marijuana vary around the world. Uruguay legalized marijuana use in 2013. In Japan, the punishment for using marijuana is up to five years in prison. According to U.S. federal law, use or possession of marijuana is illegal. Still, many U.S. states have legalized some forms of the drug. Technically, state laws cannot go against federal laws. But as of 2017, federal officials have not stopped states from legalizing marijuana.

Peoples' opinions about marijuana differ greatly. Some people believe all marijuana use is dangerous. They think the drug should be illegal. Others believe marijuana should be legal for medical use only. Some people want to legalize both medical and recreational marijuana.

Americans who use marijuana in states where it is legal are still breaking the federal law. For this reason, supporters of marijuana want to legalize it at both the federal and state levels.

U.S. Marijuana Laws by State (2018)

Beginning in 1996, many U.S. states have legalized medical marijuana. Since 2012, some states have legalized recreational marijuana as well.

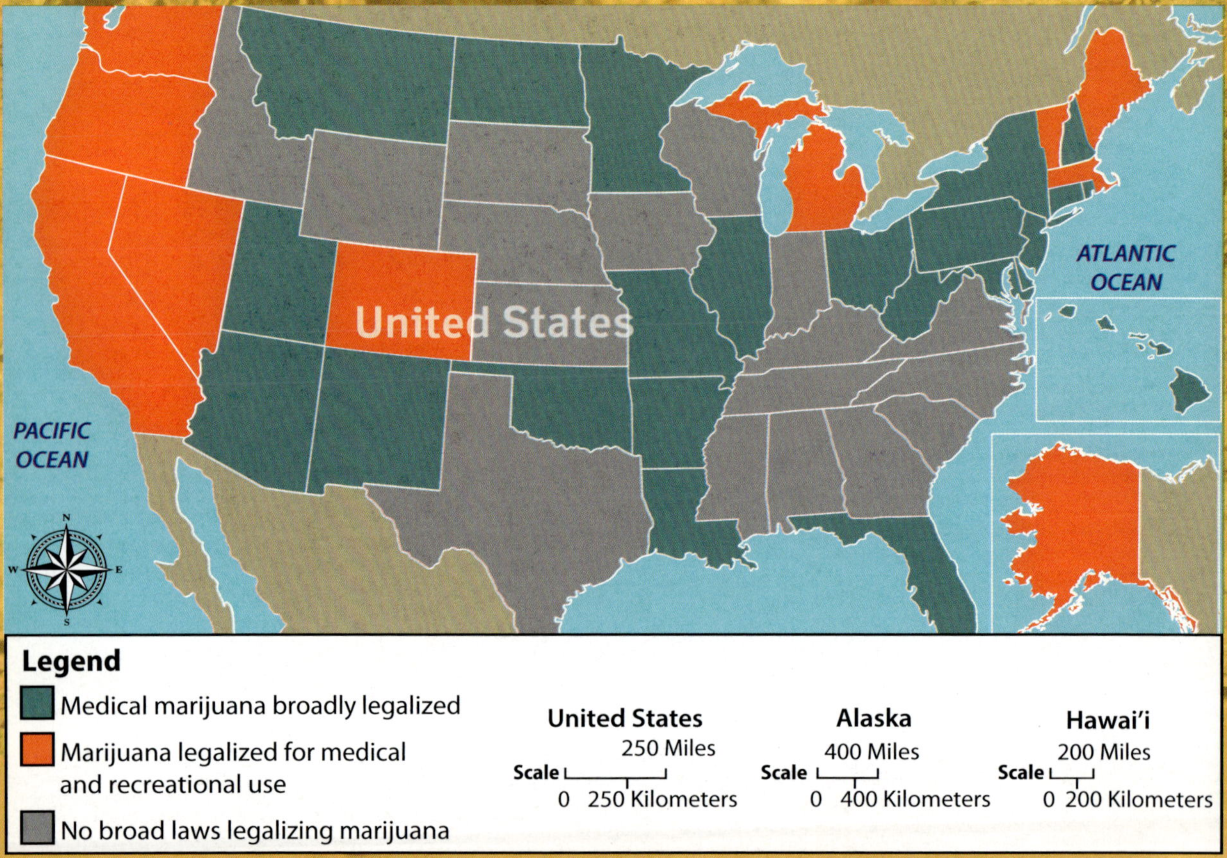

Timeline

2737 BC
Chinese emperor Shen Nung documents the use of cannabis as a medical drug.

1545 AD
Spaniards introduce cannabis to the Americas when they import it to Chile.

1937
Samuel R. Caldwell becomes one of the first people in the United States to be convicted of selling marijuana.

1985
Dronabinol, a synthetic form of a chemical found in marijuana, is approved for the treatment of nausea and vomiting in U.S. cancer patients.

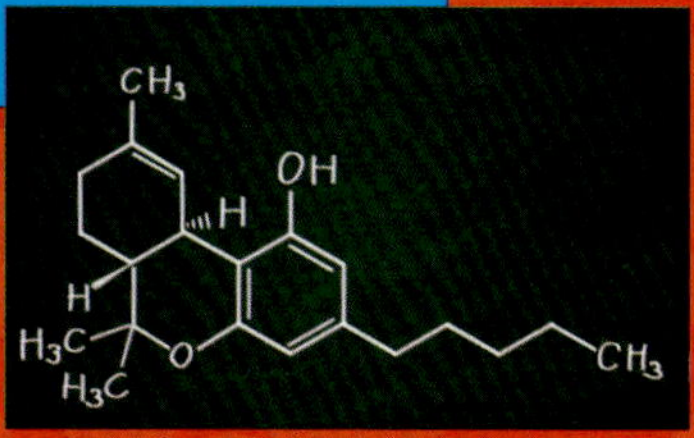

2000s
Eight U.S. states legalize medical marijuana.

2018
Canada fully legalizes recreational marijuana. It is the second country to do so.

PRO

Bhang milk is an Indian drink made with marijuana. It is often used for healing purposes.

Marijuana Has Medical Value

Medical marijuana can take several forms. Some examples are cigarettes, sprays, oils, and lotions. Tetrahydrocannabinol (THC) and Cannabidiol (CBD) are chemicals in marijuana. THC changes how the brain works, causing the user to feel high. In contrast, CBD does not cause a high.

In many cases, the chemicals in marijuana can help patients feel better. For instance, cancer patients often deal with nausea and tiredness. These symptoms are caused by **chemotherapy**. Some patients do not feel like eating. Doctors may prescribe marijuana in these cases. THC can stop nausea and increase patients' appetites.

FDA Approval

The U.S. Food and Drug Administration (FDA) must approve all drugs in the United States. Researchers test drugs on hundreds of people before they are approved. These tests show whether a drug is helpful, harmful, or both. In 1972, the U.S. government identified marijuana as a dangerous drug. This ruling made it difficult for researchers to fund studies on marijuana. The ruling also made it hard to obtain marijuana for research.

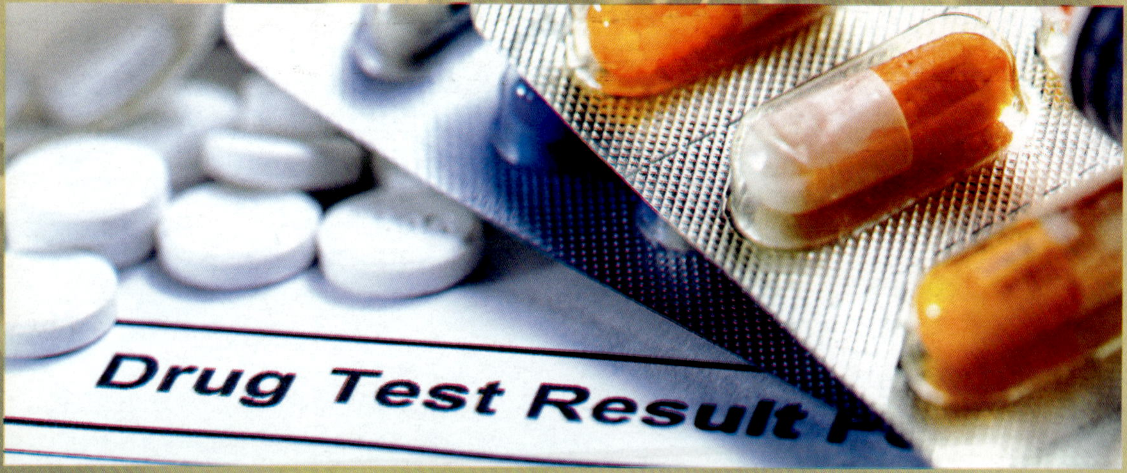

CBD oil often comes in the form of capsules.

According to animal studies, THC and CBD can slow down and kill certain cancer cells. However, scientists have not done enough human studies to know marijuana's true effects against cancer.

Doctors also use medical marijuana to treat epilepsy. Epilepsy is a disorder that causes seizures. When people have seizures, they lose control of their muscles. This can cause patients to fall and hurt themselves.

Frequent seizures can make it hard to live a normal life. Many drugs are intended to stop seizures, but they do not always work. Some patients have turned to marijuana for treatment. To treat epilepsy, scientists make CBD oil from marijuana plants. Studies show that a drug made from CBD oil can reduce seizures.

For pain relief, marijuana may be a safer alternative to **opioids**. Doctors often prescribe opioids to treat pain. However, opioids can have dangerous side effects. They can cause liver damage, brain damage, and stomach problems. In time, patients need stronger doses of opioids to relieve their pain. This can cause users to become **addicted**. They can even die from taking too large a dose. More than 49,000 people died from opioid overdose in 2017. Opioids account for more drug overdose deaths in the United States than all other drugs put together.

Studies on THC show that marijuana eases many types of pain. In 2016, doctors prescribed 1,800 fewer painkillers in states where medical marijuana was legal. And a 2014 study found that opioid overdose deaths fell by 25 percent in states with legal medical marijuana. Medical marijuana does not carry the risk of death by overdose.

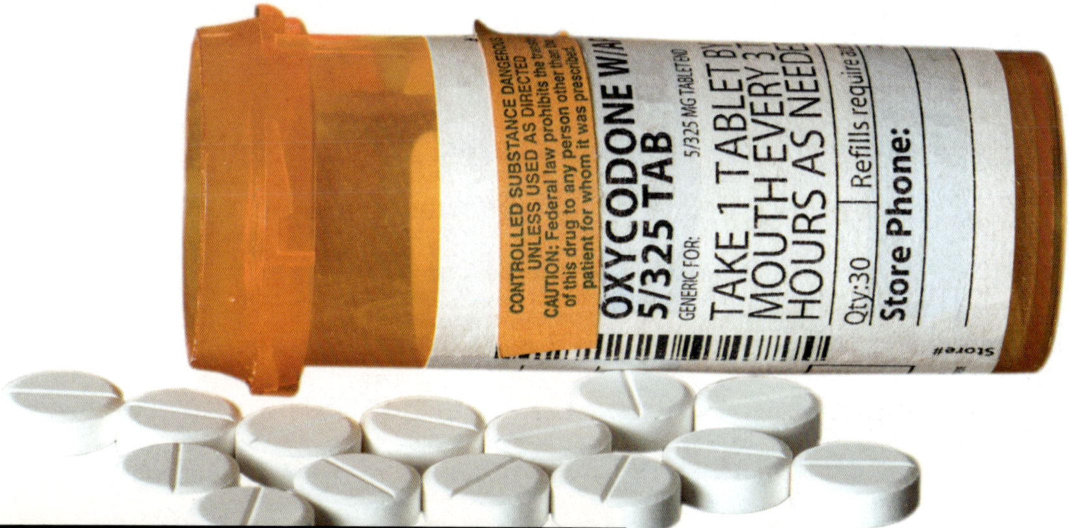

Some opioids, such as oxycodone, are legal in the United States. Others, such as heroin, are illegal.

Alcohol, which is legal in most countries, is deadlier than marijuana. In the United States, more than 2,000 people die of alcohol poisoning each year.

PRO

Morocco, Afghanistan, and Mexico are some of the world's top marijuana producers.

Legal Marijuana Can Generate Government Income

Governments use tax money to pay for public services. These services include police officers, judges, and prison workers. Arrests related to marijuana increase the need for such services. In the United States, for example, nearly half of all drug charges are related to marijuana. And each year, more than 800,000 Americans are arrested for using or possessing marijuana. Legalizing marijuana could save U.S. taxpayers nearly $8 billion per year.

Legal marijuana sales would cut into the profits of illegal dealers.

Governments spend a lot of money fighting marijuana. By legalizing the drug, governments could create extra income instead. Experts estimate that the marijuana industry generates up to $40 billion per year in the United States. But much of this money goes to illegal drug dealers. Supporters of legalization argue that money from marijuana sales should go to legal farmers and sellers. It could also go to the government.

Did You Know?

In 2012, Colorado and Washington became the first U.S. states to legalize recreational marijuana. Alaska, Oregon, and Washington, D.C., followed in 2014.

Normally, business owners pay taxes to the government. These funds help cover workers' retirement and health care plans. But when people buy and sell marijuana illegally, none of that money is taxed. Experts estimate that state taxes from legal marijuana could generate between $5 and $18 billion per year.

Taxes from marijuana sales would allow governments to increase their spending. The U.S. state of Colorado is one example. In 2012, Colorado legalized recreational marijuana. In 2017, the state earned nearly $250 million from taxes on the drug.

The CDA prevents marijuana growers from spraying plants with certain dangerous chemicals.

State officials in Colorado used the extra money to benefit citizens. They repaired old schools and built new ones. They also created educational programs to stop bullying. Other programs educated young people on the dangers of drug use. The state also provided money to the Colorado Department of Agriculture (CDA). The CDA used the funds to increase safety on marijuana farms.

In 2001 and 2003, 38 percent of surveyed adults said they tried marijuana. In a 2013 survey, that number rose to 48 percent. Supporters of legalization point out that marijuana use is on the rise. This shows that laws against marijuana do not prevent marijuana use. Legalizing marijuana would save taxpayer money. It could also create more funds for drug safety programs.

In 2016, there were **3 times** more marijuana dispensaries than **Starbucks** coffee shops in Colorado.

Every day, about **7,000** people in the United States try marijuana for the **first** time.

President Richard Nixon announced the war on drugs in 1971. Since then, the U.S. government has spent more than $1 trillion fighting illegal drug use.

PRO

Illegal dealers must secretly transport marijuana to avoid being caught.

Law Enforcement Could Focus on Violent Crimes

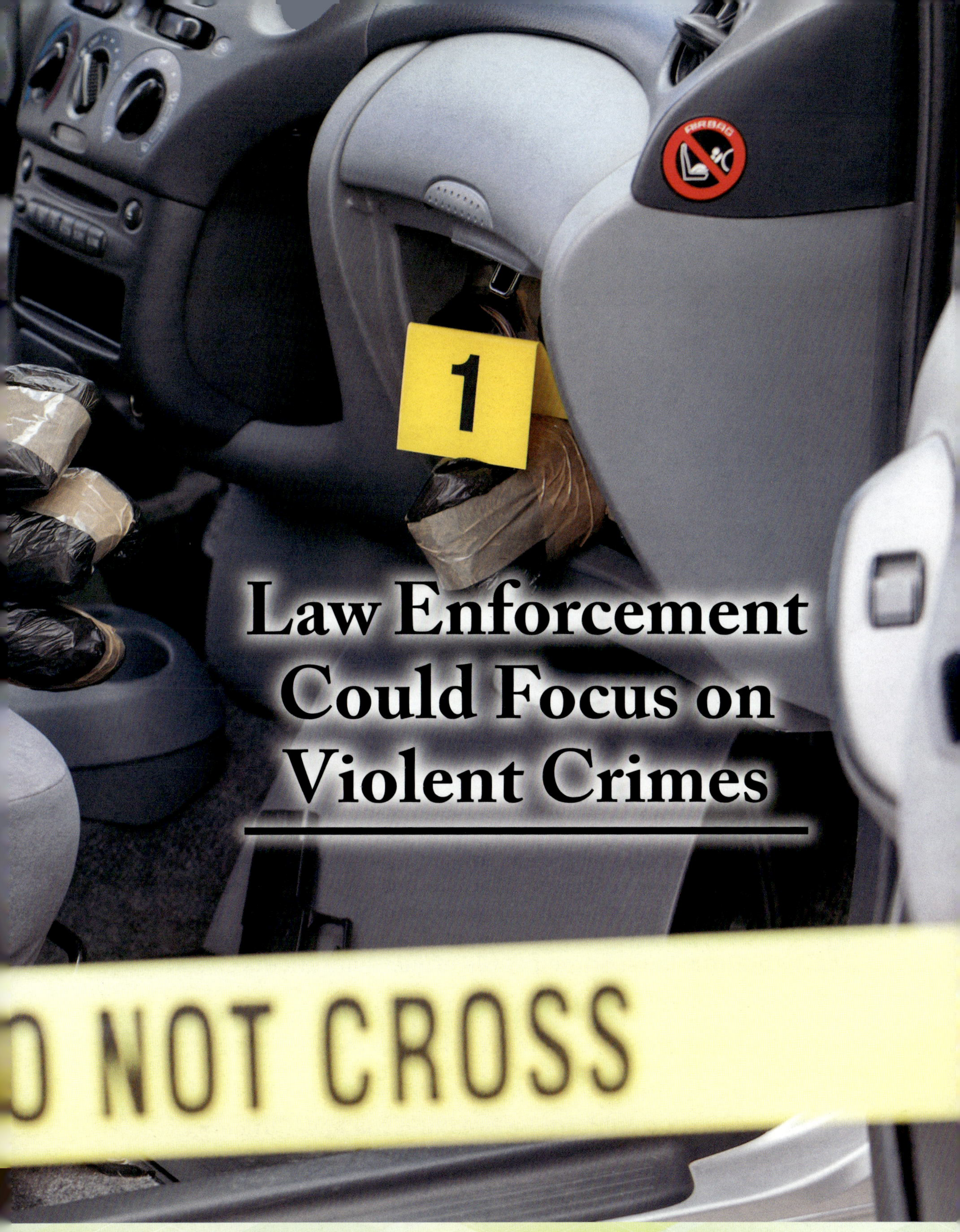

In states where marijuana is legal, marijuana dispensaries provide medical marijuana to the public.

Police officers serve an important role in the community. Their job is to protect citizens and enforce laws. Some people argue that officers spend too much time enforcing laws against marijuana. These critics want police to spend more time protecting citizens against violent crimes. If marijuana were legal, growers, sellers, and users would not be breaking the law. Officers could spend less time enforcing marijuana laws. This would give them more time to protect people from violence.

Violent crime causes physical harm to another person. Examples include assault, armed robbery, and murder. In contrast, responsible use of marijuana does not harm others. Many people consider marijuana use a victimless crime. These individuals want the police to focus on crimes that have victims.

Legalizing marijuana would also allow the government to **regulate** the marijuana industry. In states where it is legal, marijuana is sold in state-regulated shops. This means the state can control its growth, sales, and use. In Colorado, users must show identification to buy marijuana. Legal cannabis is grown on state-approved farms. This allows the government to oversee the quality of the drug. It also reduces crime connected to the illegal drug trade.

Marijuana Arrests in the United States

Between 2001 and 2010, U.S. police arrested more than 8.2 million people for marijuana-related crimes. Of these arrests, approximately 90 percent were for possession of the drug. In 2011, more arrests occurred for marijuana possession in the United States than for all violent crimes combined.

In contrast, laws against marijuana can result in dangerous industry practices. Illegal transportation of the drug across the Mexican–U.S. border causes other crimes. Violence can occur among marijuana sellers. Users may steal money so they can buy the drug. A 2017 study found that legalizing marijuana reduces such crime. In addition, U.S. medical marijuana laws have led to less violence in states that border Mexico.

U.S. Federal Penalties for Marijuana-Related Crimes

Marijuana is legal in several U.S. states. U.S. federal law, however, carries penalties for the sale or possession of marijuana.

	Maximum prison sentence	Maximum fine
Possession		
First offense (any amount)	1 year	$1,000
Second offense (any amount)	2 years	$2,500
Third offense (any amount)	3 years	$5,000
Sale or Cultivation		
Less than 50 kilograms	5 years	$250,000
50–99 kg	20 years	$1,000,000
100–999 kg	40 years	$2,000,000
1000+ kg	life	$4,000,000

According to U.S. federal law, the penalty for marijuana possession is one year in jail. Penalties for selling and growing marijuana are at least five years in jail. First-time marijuana users are put into jail with other criminals. This experience can negatively affect them. Their peers may influence them to commit more crimes in the future. After **inmates** are released, it is difficult to return to normal life. Nearly half of all inmates return to prison after being released. People with criminal records also have trouble finding jobs. Supporters of legalizing marijuana argue that there are ways other than jail to help people with drug problems.

The United States has the highest incarceration rate in the world.

CON

Marijuana is one of the most common drugs used by teenagers.

Marijuana Is Harmful to Minors

In states where recreational marijuana is legal, users must be at least 21 years old. Adults in these states make their own decisions about using the drug. Critics of legalization argue that this sends the wrong message to **minors**. They fear that young people will be influenced by adults' marijuana use. Minors might think it is okay for them to use the drug, too.

If students are caught with marijuana at school, they may be suspended or expelled.

Recreational marijuana poses many threats to minors. In the short term, THC impairs users' attention and memory. These effects can be dangerous. For instance, driving or biking while high can lead to accidents. THC also impairs users' decision-making abilities. Young people who are high might be more easily influenced by their peers. They might drink alcohol or use tobacco in response to peer pressure. Students who use marijuana might have trouble studying as well. This can affect their performance in school.

Young adults who use marijuana also risk long-term brain damage. Researchers in New Zealand tracked 1,000 people for 20 years. The participants reported their marijuana use at ages 18, 21, 26, 32, and 38. The people who used marijuana during three or more of the periods lost an average of six points on an **IQ test**.

Many marijuana sellers use warning labels to discourage use by minors.

Did You Know?

By age five or six, 95 percent of a child's brain is fully developed. The area that controls memory and mood continues to grow during a person's teenage years.

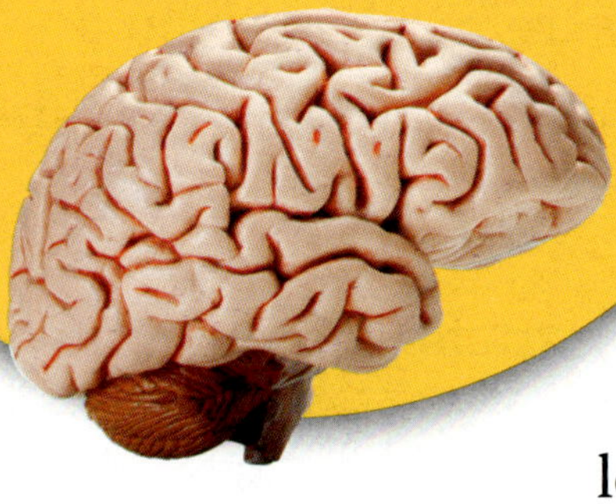

Researchers have linked teen marijuana use to other problems. For instance, many users have low grades in school. As a result, some users do not finish high school or go to college. Others have trouble finding a job. Opponents of legalization argue that marijuana use negatively affects these teens' futures.

Not all teenagers are aware of the effects of marijuana. When marijuana is legal, minors are less likely to think it is harmful. In Washington, researchers tracked teenagers' views on marijuana before and after legalization. Tenth graders' perception of the drug's harm fell by 16 percent. Parents worry that widespread legalization would have a similar effect.

High school students today are more likely to use **marijuana** than **tobacco**.

More than **40%** of U.S. teenagers have tried marijuana at least **once**.

Parents also worry about young children's access to marijuana. In places where marijuana is legal, the drug may be easier for minors to obtain. Recreational marijuana comes in many forms. Cookies, brownies, candies, and drinks can all be made with THC. These forms of marijuana are called **edibles**. Young children may mistake marijuana edibles for regular treats. If they accidentally eat them, children could become sick.

Some people eat foods containing marijuana for medical purposes.

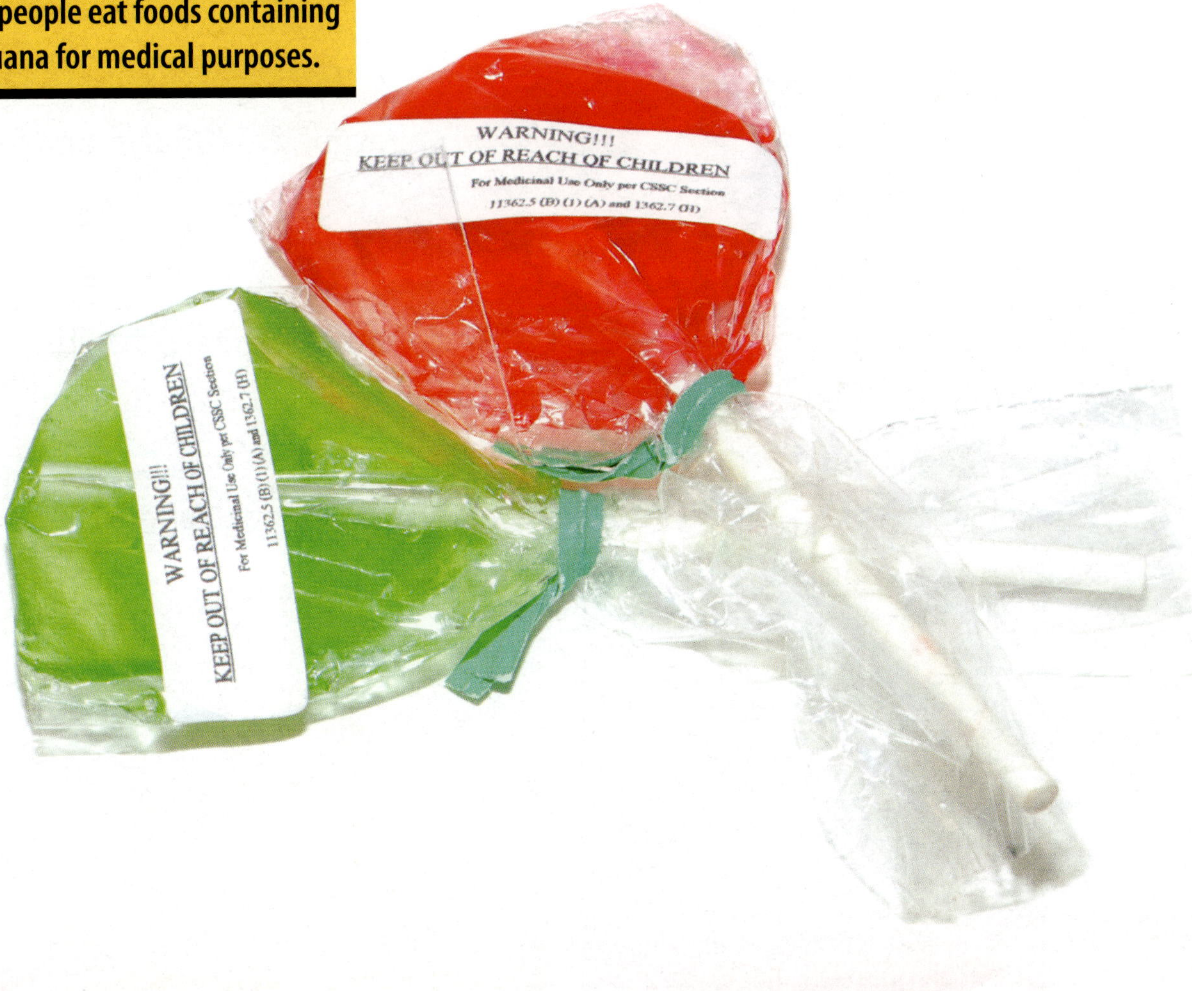

CON

Driving under the influence of alcohol or drugs puts others' lives in danger.

Driving Under the Influence of Marijuana Is Dangerous

More than 37,000 U.S. citizens die in auto accidents each year. And nearly 2.4 million people are injured in crashes. Driving under the influence of any drug is illegal. Many people argue that legalizing marijuana would lead to more accidents.

Colorado's "Drive High, Get a DUI" campaign warns drivers against drugged driving.

THC harms users' judgment, coordination, and reaction times. These effects make driving unsafe. THC is the second-most-common drug found in blood tests of crashed drivers. A driver under the influence of THC is approximately twice as likely as a sober driver to cause a deadly accident. Scientists say the exact role of marijuana in auto accidents is unclear. But critics of legalization believe enough evidence connects marijuana use with car accidents.

In 2015, drunk drivers caused approximately one-third of car accident deaths in the United States. These statistics show that drunk driving is very dangerous. Driving under the influence of both alcohol and THC is even more dangerous. When people use marijuana and drink alcohol at the same time, more THC enters the blood. Legalizing marijuana would make it easier for drivers to combine the two drugs. Some people fear this would lead to more accidents.

Conflicting Reports

The U.S. state of Washington legalized recreational marijuana in 2012. One study showed that deaths from marijuana-related crashes rose by nearly 50 percent between 2013 and 2014. However, another study found that deaths from marijuana-related crashes in Colorado and Washington did not increase. People on both sides of the argument agree that more research is needed.

Researchers are working to develop a portable device that can detect THC.

In places where marijuana is illegal, people typically use marijuana in secret. They tend to stay home to avoid the police. Using marijuana at home helps keep the public safe. Some worry that this would change with legalization. People might be more likely to use marijuana outside of their homes. This would increase their likelihood of driving under the influence.

Officers may use trained police dogs to detect marijuana in vehicles.

Legalizing marijuana would also make it harder to enforce safe driving. Identifying drivers who are under the influence of THC can be difficult. Sometimes, police officers smell or see marijuana in the car. But other times, signs of marijuana are not obvious. The driver might have smoked the marijuana in a different location. Or he or she might have eaten an edible form of the drug.

Officers must bring drivers to the police station to test for THC. However, the results of these tests are not always helpful. The drivers' THC levels can drop by the time they take the test. Police departments are searching for better ways to identify drivers under the influence of THC. Critics of legalization consider this a reason to keep marijuana illegal.

Gateway drugs, such as cigarettes, may seem harmless to users at first.

Marijuana Use Leads to More Harmful Drug Abuse

Peer pressure can lead teens to try drugs they would not otherwise use.

Some experts believe marijuana is a gateway drug. Gateway drugs lead users to use more dangerous drugs. Examples of gateway drugs include alcohol and **nicotine**. Most people do not start off using heroin or cocaine. These are extremely dangerous substances. More often, drug users begin with a beer or cigarette. After that, they might try some form of marijuana. In time, users become used to feeling high. They may then turn to stronger drugs.

Research shows that most high school students who use illegal drugs tried marijuana first. The effects of THC may make other drugs more attractive to teens. But studies also show that many teens who try marijuana do not try other drugs. Therefore, marijuana does not always act as a gateway drug.

Still, opponents of legalization think the risk is too high. They want to prevent teens from trying more harmful drugs.

Marijuana has different effects on different people. Smoking it makes some people feel good. Others do not like the way it makes them feel. Studies show that people who regularly use marijuana often feel sad or worried. These individuals lose their desire for work and play. They may feel bad about themselves. To feel better, they might try stronger drugs. Critics of legalization want to prevent this from happening.

Crystal meth is one of the most dangerous recreational drugs in the world.

Did You Know?

Most U.S. teenagers do not try marijuana. However, one in six people who start using as teens becomes addicted, according to the National Institute on Drug Abuse.

Social factors also cause marijuana to act as a gateway drug. People who try marijuana may have friends who use other drugs. These friends might encourage marijuana users to try more dangerous substances. This could lead them to form unhealthy addictions.

Some studies of gateway drugs look at cigarettes, alcohol, and marijuana at the same time. This makes it hard to know the effects of marijuana alone. Therefore, researchers are not positive that marijuana is a gateway drug. Other factors could be involved. Still, there is a **correlation** between marijuana use and more harmful drug abuse. Research shows that young people who use cocaine and heroin usually use marijuana as well. Because of this pattern, many people argue that marijuana is bad for public health.

Pros and Cons Summary

PROS

- Medical marijuana can ease side effects of chemotherapy and symptoms of epilepsy.
- Marijuana is a safe alternative to more dangerous painkillers.
- Legalizing marijuana would help governments cut spending on law enforcement.
- The government could use taxes from legal marijuana sales to benefit the public.
- Legalizing marijuana would allow police officers to focus on violent crimes.
- Legalizing marijuana would protect users from the negative effects of prison.

CONS

- Recreational marijuana negatively affects physical and mental development.
- If marijuana were legal, more children might accidentally eat marijuana edibles.
- THC impairs users' ability to drive, causing more car crashes.
- Drinking alcohol while using marijuana causes more THC to enter the blood.
- Most teenagers who use illegal drugs used marijuana first.
- Marijuana users may turn to stronger drugs for increased effects.

Marijuana Map

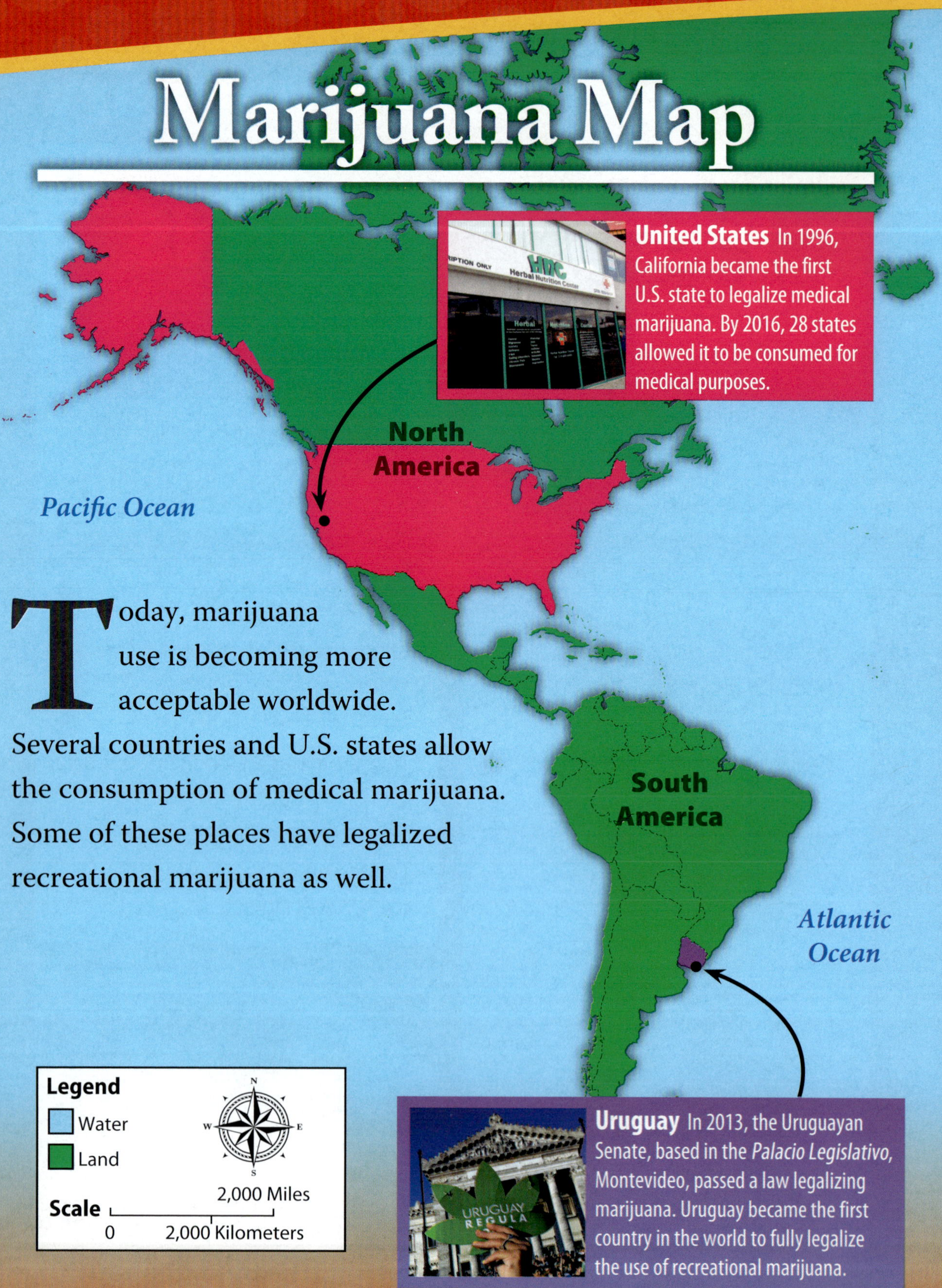

United States In 1996, California became the first U.S. state to legalize medical marijuana. By 2016, 28 states allowed it to be consumed for medical purposes.

Today, marijuana use is becoming more acceptable worldwide. Several countries and U.S. states allow the consumption of medical marijuana. Some of these places have legalized recreational marijuana as well.

Uruguay In 2013, the Uruguayan Senate, based in the *Palacio Legislativo*, Montevideo, passed a law legalizing marijuana. Uruguay became the first country in the world to fully legalize the use of recreational marijuana.

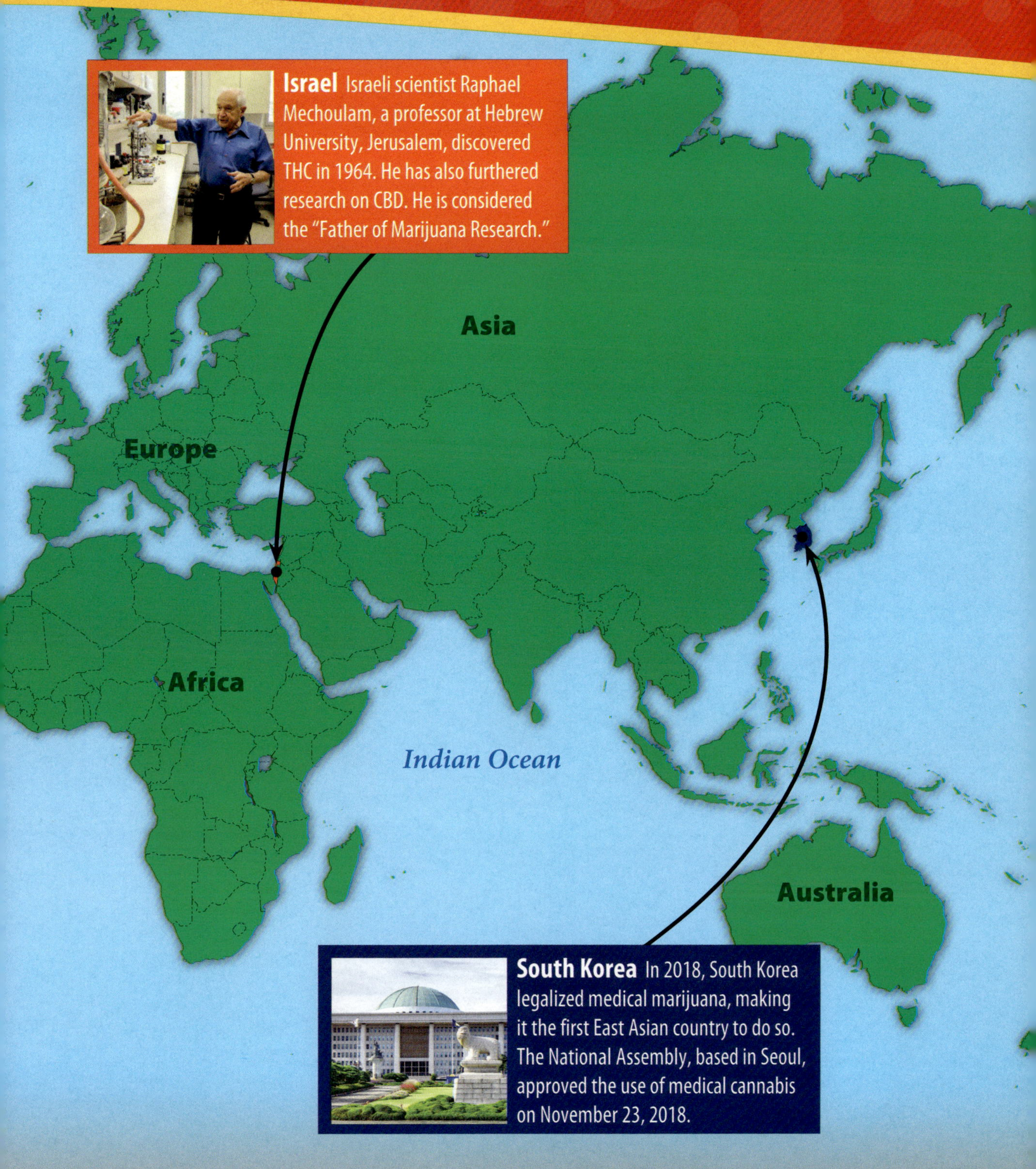

Israel Israeli scientist Raphael Mechoulam, a professor at Hebrew University, Jerusalem, discovered THC in 1964. He has also furthered research on CBD. He is considered the "Father of Marijuana Research."

South Korea In 2018, South Korea legalized medical marijuana, making it the first East Asian country to do so. The National Assembly, based in Seoul, approved the use of medical cannabis on November 23, 2018.

Quiz

1 How many chemicals does the cannabis plant contain?

2 What are two of the main chemical compounds in marijuana?

3 Which symptoms can marijuana help cancer patients with?

4 Which federal agency must approve the use of all drugs in the United States?

5 How much is the U.S. marijuana industry worth?

6 Which were the first two U.S. states to legalize recreational marijuana?

7 What are some extremely harmful recreational drugs?

8 What are some examples of possible gateway drugs?

ANSWERS **1.** More than 400 **2.** THC and CBD **3.** Nausea and loss of appetite **4.** U.S. Food and Drug Administration (FDA) **5.** About $40 billion a year **6.** Colorado and Washington **7.** Cocaine, crystal meth, and heroin **8.** Alcohol, nicotine, and marijuana

Key Words

addicted: having a physical need to use a drug regularly

chemotherapy: the use of chemical substances to kill cancer cells

correlation: a relationship between one thing and another

edibles: things that can be eaten

inmates: people who are confined to a prison

IQ test: a test that measures a person's level of intelligence

minors: people under the age of official adulthood and legal responsibility

nicotine: a toxic and addictive drug that is found in tobacco

opioids: natural or synthetic drugs derived from the opium poppy plant

prescribe: to recommend a treatment or medication to someone who is sick

recreational: done for fun and enjoyment

regulate: to control or maintain

Index

Log on to www.av2books.com

AV² by Weigl brings you media enhanced books that support active learning. Go to www.av2books.com, and enter the special code found on page 2 of this book. You will gain access to enriched and enhanced content that supplements and complements this book. Content includes video, audio, weblinks, quizzes, a slide show, and activities.

AV² Online Navigation

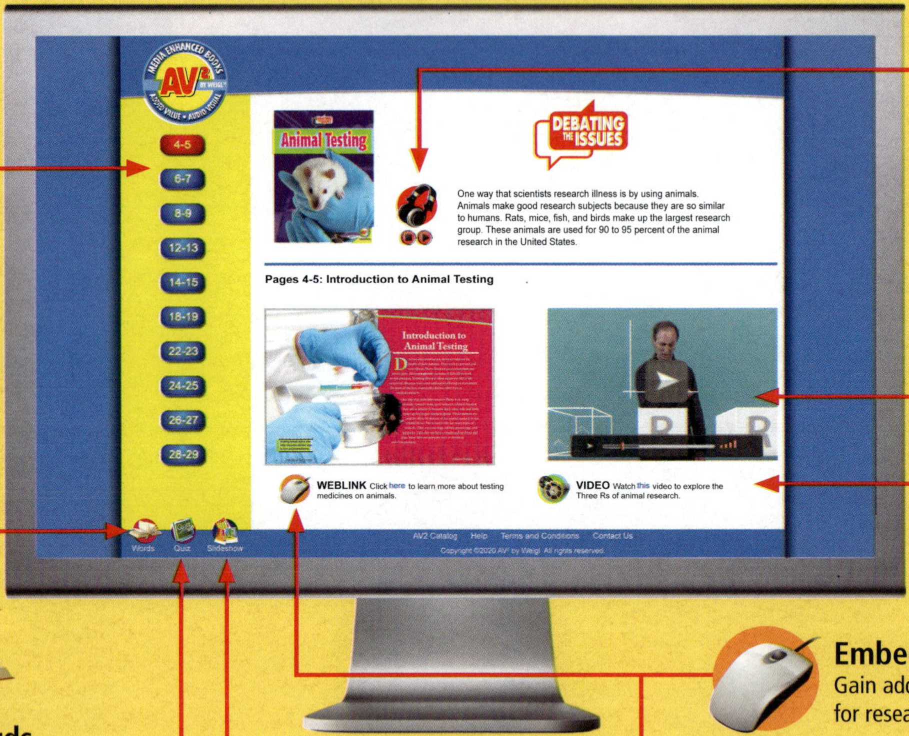

Audio
Listen to sections o the book read alou

Book Pages
AV² pages directly correspond to pages in the book.

Video
Watch informative video clips.

Embedded Weblinks
Gain additional information for research.

Key Words
Study vocabulary, and complete a matching word activity.

Try This!
Complete activities and hands-on experiments.

Quizzes
Test your knowledge.

Slide Show
View images and captions, and prepare a presentation.

AV² was built to bridge the gap between print and digital. We encourage you to tell us what you like and what you want to see in the future.

Sign up to be an AV² Ambassador at www.av2books.com/ambassador.

Due to the dynamic nature of the Internet, some of the URLs and activities provided as part of AV² by Weigl may have changed or ceased to exist. AV² by Weigl accepts no responsibility for any such changes. All media enhanced books are regularly monitored to update addresses and sites in a timely manner. Contact AV² by Weigl at 1-866-649-3445 or av2books@weigl.com with any questions, comments, or feedback.